Advance Praise

"I had the good fortune of witnessing Reverend Wild's gifts firsthand when she was invited to conduct a series of spiritually healing séances with a group of my patients who were addressing issues of trauma and loss.

Even the most skeptical later described a peaceful comfort from engaging with the spirit world, and requested additional séances. Reverend Wild brought a remarkable wisdom and sensitivity that can only come from personal experience, to create a safe and healing experience for all of the participants. Authenticity, strength, and creativity were a few of the adjectives that my patients used to describe her. One compared her to the steadiness of the Earth, solid with only the crust visible but containing great power.

Wild's work is accessible on multiple levels whether you are an adherent of Spiritualism, a believer in Jungian archetypes, of magic and shamanism, or simply an unbeliever with an open mind.

Enjoy this journey with a wonderfully capable guide."

- Nancy Oliveri, LCSW Psychotherapy

The Art of Forgiveness

*How to Get Past It
Without Letting Anyone Off the Hook*

THE ART
OF
forgiveness

HOW TO GET PAST IT
WITHOUT LETTING ANYONE
OFF THE HOOK

Reverend Stephanie Wild

NEW YORK

LONDON • NASHVILLE • MELBOURNE • VANCOUVER

The Art of Forgiveness

How to Get Past It Without Letting Anyone Off the Hook

Published in New York, New York, by Morgan James Publishing in partnership with Difference Press. Morgan James is a trademark of Morgan James, LLC. www.MorganJamesPublishing.com

The Morgan James Speakers Group can bring authors to your live event. For more information or to book an event visit The Morgan James Speakers Group at www.TheMorganJamesSpeakersGroup.com.

ISBN 9781683507659 paperback
ISBN 9781683507666 eBook
Library of Congress Control Number: 2017914172

Cover Design by:
Megan Whitney

Interior Design by:
Paul Curtis

In an effort to support local communities, raise awareness and funds, Morgan James Publishing donates a percentage of all book sales for the life of each book to Habitat for Humanity Peninsula and Greater Williamsburg.

Get involved today! Visit
www.MorganJamesBuilds.com

This book is dedicated to my spirit guides
who have been with me all along,
though I didn't always know it or believe it.
Also, to N, K, J, and W, who trusted me
and made me better.

Contents

Introduction

My [Short] Story

My journey to forgiveness began at the age of 6, when I was first abused by my father. I immediately began to look for reasons why it had happened to me. There was no way I could be happy until I had the answer. I couldn't let it go. The answer was not to be found in my home, nor to be found at school. I couldn't even find it at church.

I kept searching into my 20s. I didn't find the answer at the bottom of a bottle, or in the beds of the many men I met, or in existentialist French literature. Though I tried them all, and more. Life was bleak, and suicide was attractive. People told me I should forgive my father (and my mother for her complicity) to be happy. I couldn't imagine ever doing that. I thought it meant believing that what they did was acceptable; believing that it was OK for them to have put their perverted needs before the integrity of my body and my mind and my spirit; believing that it was OK for them to have used me rather than respect me as a human being and not treat me like their property. Perhaps you're feeling similarly.

More than 10 years of therapy took me through my 30s and helped me untangle the knots of my psyche. After what I had been through, I still had to be the one to do the hard work. I got to know my emotions intimately. I got to know my thoughts as they ran around in my brain, yelling at me. I came to understand why I behaved the way I did; how my behaviors had protected me as a child and how they were hurting me now.

But I still didn't understand why the abuse had happened. I had been a child. I hadn't deserved such betrayal. And I could not believe that it was random and meaningless.

The only place left to explore was the metaphysical realm. I had exhausted logic and analysis. Thus, all my searching, all my research, all my experimenting led me to the world of Spirit. I am not one for blind faith. Not after having lived in the center of a filthy black lie for all of my young life. So, I approached the metaphysical world with a curious, open, but still analytical mind. I wanted evidence.

I studied intuition, consciousness, and metaphysics in earnest. Little by little, the connection between Body and Soul was revealed to me. And I was led to Spiritualism. A science, a philosophy, and a religion. Not a religion that requires blind faith, but a religion that encourages personal investigation and personal connection to Infinite Intelligence.

The principles and practice of Spiritualism explained everything and I found my answer to the question, "Why?": The experience of living in our physical bodies allows us to test universal spiritual principles like Cause and Effect (some people call it Karma) and Pure Love. And that is why we go through everything we do on Earth. We are not physical beings having a spiritual experience, but spiritual beings having a physical (and emotional) experience. Earth School is an intensive learning experience.

Eventually, I was called by God (or whatever you want to call it) to become ordained as a Spiritualist Minister. It is in that capacity that I write this book for you.

Very often, forgiveness was a topic of contemplation, conversation, and meditation for me. As I became more peaceful and more serene, I would turn to myself and ask myself, "Have you forgiven?" One day, the answer was, "Yes." And so, I looked back and figured out what I had done. That process is laid out for you here, in this book. You must make the journey, but I hope I can make it easier and faster for you.

Just Get Over It

Have you ever been told to just let it go? Just move on. Just get over it; get past it. Stop carrying that around with you. I had. But what I hadn't been told was how.

One of the first few people I told about the abuse I experienced was a college friend of mine. She shared that her dad had played "rough stuff" with her, throwing her head first into the sofa at home and so on. I shared that my dad did something similar, but with a more sexual flavor–he would put me into wrestling holds like "the Boston crab." I still don't know if that's an actual wrestling move. The years went on, we partied together, gossiped together, commiserated over boys together, and then, when we were about 25, I brought up the abuses we had suffered once again. She told me, "Just let it go, Steph."

I said, "But how? What did you do?"

I was sitting on the floor at the end of her bed. I had run away from home, finally. I had driven across the country with my boyfriend of the time, and I was desperately trying to find happiness. It was late afternoon. The sun was warm and gentle through her sheer curtains.

She smiled at me and she handed me a little cartoon book. I took it with the yearning of a woman dying of thirst. I thought I would finally have the solution.

I opened the book. It started off with a young woman being sad and antisocial and always complaining. (Yes, that was me alright.) Her friends got sick of her. (Yes, I was about at that point.) She was carrying this big heavy burden. (Yes, absolutely.) Then she let her burden go. She was lighter and more congenial. She wasn't weighed down anymore. Voila! Happiness.

I looked back up at my friend, and said again, "But how?"

"Just read the book," she said.

"I just read the book!" I had learned how to speed read at age 13. "It says to let go, but it doesn't say how! I mean, what did you actually do?"

"I just let it go," she said.

I was infuriated. "So I'm supposed to just let it go? Like, instantly?"

She nodded and smiled.

"That's ridiculous," I said.

"You've got to let it go, Steph."

"I can't just decide to let it go. And then it's magically done. I mean. First of all, what is 'it'?"

"Keep the book," she said.

"I don't need the book—it doesn't tell me anything useful."

She wasn't the only one who expected me to be able to just get over it. A teacher of mine did, too. He mentioned a movie and asked if I'd seen it. I said yes, I'd really liked it. (Truth be told, I found it very hard to concentrate on movies and TV shows, as I was plagued by intrusive thoughts.) Anyway, he said he wondered what I had thought about the lead character and how she had become much happier once she had "lifted off that yoke."

I told him, "Yeah, it's not that easy. That was a movie."

For a long time I searched out the meaning of forgiveness. I answered the door to Mormons who told me, "The Lord forgives," but couldn't tell me how I could do it, too. I read book after book that described forgiveness as "choosing to let go of anger and bitterness." Yes, but how?

How to Get Past It: Forgiveness

I am sure that if we could, we would all "just let it go"; let it fall into the Grand Canyon; the deep blue sea; the depths of hell. But what is "it"? It's not a thing. It's not a cursed mirror that we can throw into the magical healing stream. It's not an ancient wooden box containing our sorrow that we can throw off the holy mountain. "It" is a spiritual wound.

Healing this spiritual wound is a spiritual process. This spiritual process is called forgiveness. Forgiveness is not an intellectual exercise: We cannot simply decide to forgive and feel free. The result of forgiveness is freedom from anger and resentment. The result of forgiveness is peace and serenity and joy. The result of forgiveness is mastery of one's own happiness.

Every spiritual teacher will tell you that forgiveness is key to happiness. But even the great spiritual teachers, most of them, end up describing what forgiveness is and not how to do it. And even when they do describe how to do it, the description is layered and complex and opaque—more poetry than instruction manual. That's lovely; and meditating and musing and mulling over it all (together with cognitive behavioral therapy and body work) has brought me, eventually, to recovery.

But it was a haphazard, incoherent, heart-wrenching, lonely, terrifying journey. One that I was not sure would ever actually end; one that I was not sure I would survive with my sanity.

It doesn't have to be so horrifying and difficult for you. I have figured it out and set it down on paper and I want to share it with you. I can support you every step of the way. For me, it has taken 40 years. But don't despair; now that I understand exactly how to do it, I can help you do it much more quickly.

Still, healing this spiritual wound happens over time. The wound is deep, and we must go layer by layer. And still, it will be messy—emotions, memories, and physical sensations surface so that they can be released. The journey is not for the faint of heart. I know you have the courage, but it's also essential to have a spiritual support system and to acquire a set of spiritual tools to make you safe and feel loved. This book will give you the tools and, if you wish, I can be part of your spiritual support system.

How to Get Past It Without Letting Anyone Off the Hook

I would like you to benefit from what I have learned. To have you understand your own emotions, thoughts, and behaviors; to get a sense of why the abuse or trauma happened to you and how you can get past it without letting anyone off the hook.

Yes, it is completely possible to get past resentment and anger–to forgive–without compassion for your abusers and those who were complicit. You do not have to understand their point of view. We are not saints.

You are not responsible for your abuser's feelings anymore. Or their reputation. You are not responsible for the feelings or the reputation of anyone who was complicit. You do not have to spend time in their company if you do not want to. You do not have to do what they say or love them or like them or pretend that you do. You do not have to be friendly with your abusers or those who were complicit; you do not have to have any contact with them; not even family occasions; you do not have to save them from embarrassment. It is their job to reckon with what they have done. You owe them exactly nothing. You only owe yourself happiness.

So, to get past it–to complete the process of forgiveness and reach happiness, there are just three things to do:

- Accept the present. That means accepting that the abuse happened, that it cannot be undone, and that it is affecting you right now. It means you must accept your emotions, memories, and physical sensations as they are and as they arise. These feelings may include grieving the lack of loving parents or siblings, or the loss of your innocence in a horrid way. It may include current sickness and depression. Whatever it is, you cannot deny it anymore.

- Admit you are responsible for your own happiness. You can choose happiness. You have to choose, because you have free will. Unutterably terrible things may have happened to you. The betrayal may be unfathomably deep. But the choice to pursue happiness is yours alone. The Universe cannot help you if it does not hear your cry.

- Act in your own best interests. You are responsible for your actions from here on out. You have the power to put your shoes on in the morning or not. You can choose whether to put the wine to your lips or not. No more excuses.

You don't have to do any of this alone. I am here to help. I think it is my purpose on Earth. And the Universe, which I call Infinite Intelligence, will follow your lead. You only have to set the intention for healing and hold the desire for help in your heart. Your Spirit guides, Guardian Angels, and loved ones who have crossed over will come the instant you call, as well.

How to Use This Book

I recommend reading this book in order from beginning to end. Chapters 1, 2, and 3 are about the effects of childhood abuse, especially sexual abuse. You will get several examples from my experience and some from my clients.

Chapters 1 and 2 are about accepting the present. Chapter 1 discusses the core pain of abuse: the horror, and the forces surrounding us that push us toward denial. In order to heal, we cannot deny; we must accept. So start here. Chapter 2 discusses the nature and source of the powerful and painful emotions that are the result of having suffered abuse. We must accept these emotions and process them. Suppressing these emotions leads to sickness and behaviors that damage ourselves and others.

Chapters 3 and 4 are about admitting you are responsible for your happiness:

In Chapter 3, I discuss blame and responsibility. This is a critical step—accepting responsibility—it can be easy to fool ourselves that we want to feel better when we really don't want to. We are familiar with being oppressed; being the underdog; being in pain; using this to whatever advantage we can. It takes great courage to admit we do not want pity anymore; that we want to take care of ourselves and be judged on our merits and not by our wounds. We have free will and this is where we use it consciously. Each day.

In Chapter 4, I reveal the Spiritualist point of view of life on Earth. We each have a lesson that we have chosen for ourselves, with the help of our guides. Any abuse we have experienced has a purpose. I find this notion extremely comforting. Again, if you are a nonbeliever, you can accept this as metaphor and interact with the ideas on a symbolic level.

Chapter 5 discusses the Spirit world. There is infinite solace to be had, and infinite love. You can connect to Spirit guides, Guardian Angels, loved ones who have passed, and Love itself. All are available to help and comfort you. If you are a nonbeliever but have an open mind, there is abundant evidence to be found and considered. If you still choose not to believe in an Infinite Intelligence, that is your prerogative, and this process can still serve you. I advise you to choose some higher power, because to call on a higher power means we do not have to carry the weight of the world on our shoulders. In fact, I began my spiritual journey by choosing the ocean as my higher power. Her strength and beauty were a great comfort. I would go to the beach late at night and cry and scream, and she would accept my pain and sorrow without complaint. Nothing was too much for her.

Chapter 6 puts it all together. Oftentimes, when we are triggered or just depressed or anxious on an ordinary day, we can't recall or process complex ideas. I have distilled all I have learned in my 40-year journey of forgiveness in an easy-to-remember way.

Chapter 7 provides the scientific underpinnings of the assertion that we are all connected; all one. When doubt creeps in for me, I can fall back on this evidence, rather than fall into depression or fear, and soon enough I can move forward again, knowing I am literally never alone.

Chapters 8 and 9 give you some advice on moving forward as you peel back the layers. This book provides all you really need to complete the process of forgiveness, but there are times you may feel confused or discouraged or scared or desolate. If you want someone to bear witness and support you through your journey, I am here.

Chapter 1:
Denied Reality

The First Incident

The first time I was told I couldn't trust myself, I was about five years old. I had run into my mom and dad's room when my dad got home from work, as I was so happy to see him. He was changing out of his work clothes. When I ran in, he was down to his tighty-whiteys. He took those off and started sort of airing his balls out–massaging them and bouncing them around in his right hand. Then he sniffed his fingers and shoved them under my nose.

"What is it? What's that smell?"

He grinned and said, "Do you like it?"

I felt a shiver go all up and down my little body. I hopped from foot to foot and back again. It was an entirely new sensation that this musty, musky scent had evoked in me. I was tingling "down there;" my body was electrified to the tips of my fingers. It was awful and exciting. He did it again: stuck his fingers under his balls, sniffed them, shoved them under my nose. And then the thing started to wiggle. As if by magic, it went up a bit, down a bit, up and down.

I screamed. "What is it?"

Dad laughed and snorted and I saw the gold fillings in his molars. He said, "Lick it. Lick it."

So I did. I put the tip of my tongue on the tip of the thing. It tasted briny and cool. I looked up at him. "Lick it," he said, more gruffly.

His face had changed and my dad wasn't jolly and fun. I wasn't feeling affection coming from him. I suddenly felt revolted and terrified.

"What is it?" I screamed again. He was rubbing it now. I ran out of the room, still hopping from foot to foot and back again, trying to get the terrible tingle out of me. I ran into the kitchen, just a few feet away, where my mother was standing. She was staring at the wall.

The Complicity

"What's that thing that goes up and down on Daddy?" I pleaded as I hopped around.

"What thing?"

"That thing! That thing! It goes up and down!"

"I don't know," she said, sounding annoyed.

"Yes you do!" I was starting to cry now.

She grunted air. "His penis."

"Daddy made me lick his penis."

"He did not." And there it was.

"He did!" I wanted to tell her what had just happened, what it was like, get a hug from her, and hear her explanation for my feelings. I needed some comfort and to learn from her all about this strange incident.

But instead, I got, "Don't say things like that about your father."

"Ask him!"

She called him out to the kitchen. "Neil! Neil!"

We stood there for a while. She made no effort to comfort me. I walked backward into the hallway between the kitchen and their bedroom, stewing in my tears. Eventually he came out.

"She says you made her lick your penis," my mother said, without looking at either of us.

"What?" he scoffed. "She's lying."

"I am not lying!" I was crying hard now and starting to feel terrified. "I'm not lying! I didn't even know what it was until you told me! Why don't you believe me?" No comfort was coming. The people who I thought loved me the most in the world, the people who I thought would guide me best about every feeling, every fear, every pain, were untrustworthy.

"I told you not to say things like that about your father."

I looked at my father, then, and he looked at me. I suddenly understood my vulnerability. I clearly understood my solitude. And then the moment of clarity was gone. Clarity was gone for a long, long time. And replaced with almost-madness.

The Madness

I went into my bedroom and sat down. My mind hurt. I just felt … crazy. My understanding of the world had just been turned inside out and upside down. What I thought was true, was not. What I had just experienced taught me that my parents were not going to protect me from absolute horror.

"But that could not possibly be true!" I thought. "There must be some other explanation for this."

Since real parents are not monsters, I thought, the people in my house could not be my parents. That was the only logical explanation. I must be from the faery realm. I had been read some Grimm's fairytales by my Great Aunt that explained changelings. Perhaps she knew and was secretly teaching me about my real identity. Yes. That was it. I was a changeling from the faery realm.

But why would I have been sent to these monsters? It must be some kind of test. But what was the reward? A kingdom! Yes. I was a princess! Yes, of course. I had seen princesses in storybooks, too. They all had a test to pass before they could live happily ever after.

So, from this day on, I had to be good. I had to learn the rules of this human realm and behave perfectly, so that my real faery parents would be pleased with me and come and take me back to rule my faery kingdom.

The (Never) Forgetting

As the days went by, I was a good little girl. My mother's friends always commented, "She's so well behaved! She's so good!"

The experience of that first assault melded into my daily life, and my mind did not replay the incident for a long, long time. I was about 21 when it came back to me.

But my body has never forgotten what happened; my soul has never forgotten what happened. From that moment, I was sad. I was lonely. I was listless. I was bored by everything. I found no joy in anything. I developed terrible migraines that lasted for days. I had crippling anxiety almost 24 hours a day. I had night terrors. I played sexualized games with friends and had sexual torture fantasies. I was vulnerable to other people who could sense that I wanted love and approval; they abused me (mostly emotionally), too.

As the years went by there were other assaults from my father. And always complicity from my mother. The actual touching didn't stop until I was about 14, when I told him directly never to touch me again. But he still watched me in the shower, he still made comments on my body, he still masturbated at me while I slept. Then at about 15, I started drinking alcohol, so I lived in temporary oblivion and it was all much, much easier to forget.

The Remembering

The first flashback came when I was sitting by the pool in my parents' house. The house I had lived in from the age of eight. I was drinking Drambuie with a college friend since my parents were away. It was our first year of law school. We were sitting on a lounger with a very bright blue cushion; the blue was so bright it hurt my eyes. It was a cloudy day with a humid breeze. I had had several large gulps of Drambuie, and suddenly I saw it. A picture in my mind. A picture of my dad and his penis and me and my tongue.

I turned my head sharply to the right and said, "Oh, my God." My friend asked, "What?"

I said, "I just remembered something. But it can't be true." He said, "What?"

I said, "I don't even want to say. Don't worry."

The First Step

And that was the beginning of the reckoning. More and more memories came to the forefront of my mind. I suppose my soul knew it was time to deal with it. I felt strangely calm in these first weeks. More madness and despair would come later. But for now, my hatred of my parents, my cynicism, my tough exterior, my wild behavior, and everything else, made sense.

Several months later, I was staying with a crew of friends at a house on the beach. The anxiety had been building. I felt I would burst if I didn't tell. I asked one of them to stay up with me after the others went to bed because I had something I needed to tell him. This guy had always been sweet and kind to me and had never made any sexual overtures even though he loved me. He is still a friend.

We had all been drinking, as usual. He asked me if it was OK if another friend listened too. He sensed what was coming, and he didn't want to hear it all on his own. And he wanted me to feel even more supported.

I said, "I've been having flashbacks. Memories that I had forgotten. My dad sexually abused me."

My love said, "We believe you, Steph. We believe you."

"Really?" I said.

"Yes! And it's not your fault."

It had never occurred to me that it was my fault, really. I was just blind with anger and confusion and sorrow. I understood later that even though, intellectually, I always knew it was not my fault, I had behaved as if it were–I had turned against myself, hurting myself with promiscuity, drinking, anger, and so on.

I said to my two friends, "Thank you. Thank you. Thank you."

I felt relieved. I thought that this might be the cure. I hoped that telling it and crying over it would cure me. It didn't. But it was the beginning of taking care of myself. It was the beginning of trusting my instincts, my emotions, my Self. It was the first step of my spiritual healing.

You Are Not Crazy

I want you to know, dear reader, that I believe you. The abuse happened. It happened as you remember it. Your emotions and your physical sensations happened just as you say they did. I believe you. I don't "believe that you believe it." I simply believe you. You had that experience. Those who told you it did not happen the way you say are protecting their own sanity at the expense of yours. They are selfish and afraid. We will talk about them more, later. For now, know that I understand. And know that you can trust your emotions, your body, your Self.

REFLECTION

- Were there times you were taught that what you experienced was not reality? (for example, your abuser telling you it didn't hurt, didn't happen, or didn't happen the way you remembered)

- How did your body remember and communicate the abuse to you? (for example, headaches, extra weight, sexual preferences)

- How did your soul remember and communicate the abuse to you? (for example, depression, anger, thrill seeking)

- When was the first time someone believed you about your abuser? How did you feel in your body when that happened? How did you feel in your soul?

- Have you ever thought or been told that you "should just get over it"?

Chapter 2:
Denied Emotions

The Psychosomatic System

Our soul (or mind, if you prefer that term) speaks to us through our thoughts, which cause our emotions, which we feel in our body. Consciously or unconsciously, our mind manifests in various parts of the body. This is not a metaphor. Actual molecules of emotion run every system in our body.

Neuropeptides: The Molecules of Emotion

Scientists call molecules of emotion neuropeptides. Intelligence in the form of neuropeptides and their receptors (which they use to communicate with our cells) are in the brain and all throughout the body.

Each emotion is associated with a particular neuropeptide or combination of neuropeptides. In order for you to feel an emotion, your brain (specifically, the part of the brain called the hypothalamus) has to create and release a set of neuropeptides. Each emotion has its own particular set of neuropeptides, its own chemical combination. The neuropeptides give you the experience of that emotion.

First, you have a thought, like, "Oh no, he's going to touch me," or "That look means she doesn't want me to say anything," then your hypothalamus transforms that thought into neuropeptides and you feel an emotion. Neuropeptides are also released via the "memory" of cells around the body. In this way, your thoughts create your reality.

Specific neuropeptides are involved with specific emotions. For example, norepinephrine, one kind of neuropeptide, flows in happy states of mind. But get this: Norepinephrine uses a certain receptor to enter each cell. The reovirus, a cause of the common cold, uses the same receptor to enter each cell. So presumably, when you're happy, the virus can't enter the cell because the norepinephrine is already occupying the receptors. Cultivate happiness and you avoid getting sick. Cool, right?

All Emotions Are Positive Emotions

It's not just a matter of thinking happy thoughts, though. Since any emotional expression is always tied to a flow of peptides, the chronic repression of emotions results in a massive disturbance of the psychosomatic network. If the energy of an emotion is not released, it will cause damage.

Not expressing emotions–any emotion, whether "positive" or "negative"–creates blockages and slows the flow of peptide signals that maintain function at the cellular level. This weakened system may lead to adverse effects in our bodies, and even serious disease. So letting "dark" emotions flow is just as important as cultivating "light" emotions. All emotions are positive emotions when we let them flow.

We tried to meet the needs of our abusers and their accomplices by not expressing our real feelings about the abuse, by not expressing the feelings that the abuse created. We may have kept our emotions secret to save their sanity; to protect their social positions; to keep the family together; to protect our delicate child's ego, or for many other reasons we were told directly or subtly. For me, it was all of these things. And for all of us, it has adverse effects.

Emotions Drive Behaviors

When the receptors for a specific neuropeptide are stimulated over and over again, the body creates more receptors for that neuropeptide. They replicate more quickly than other cells. Now the body wants that higher level of specific neuropeptide to connect to all the receptors. So, we go in search of it. Our bodies have become addicted to a certain neuropeptide: a certain emotion.

We get ourselves into situations that make us feel the emotion the receptors need. These situations will often be re-enactments of the abuse, because we know for certain that we can get the emotions that way. Other receptors that are not used can die off, so we don't even feel those emotions very much anymore. We can retrain our brain at any age, though, do not despair. Again, the key is to express whatever emotion comes up to avoid blockage and keep the peptides flowing. Accept it, express it, release it.

For example, a common behavior for women who have been sexually abused in childhood is promiscuity and getting into romantic relationships with abusive men. Therapists will call this "acting out." I never quite understood why I was doing that. Why was I acting out the abusive scenario? I was smarter than that!

My client Amanda felt the same way. The explanation is that we are addicted, if you will, to those neuropeptides; we have been conditioned to seek out this nasty kind of sexual and relational experience to get them.

Amanda, in trying to take control of her body, decided to try out being a dominatrix. She figured it was a way to own her sexuality, take out some anger on men, and make some quick money. But it didn't bring her comfort. A small amount of satisfaction, yes. And some money, yes. But it made her feel shame and disgust, like when she was abused by her uncle.

Her boss didn't allow drinking while working with the clients, so, unable to anaesthetize herself, she ended up being aware of these emotions she was having and staying spiritually present for them. I coached her to consciously let them flow in the moment (she could actually use them in her work, so they did not disrupt her potential to earn money). I channeled healing energy to her, to fill the void that releasing the shame and disgust had created. In a matter of a month or so, Amanda decided she didn't want to put herself in that situation anymore; she didn't feel the need to create those emotions anymore.

But shame is powerful. Now she felt ashamed that she had worked in the sex industry! And of course, our society encouraged that shame. As we talked, she accepted the shame that came up, released it, and welcomed feelings lying beneath.

Layer by layer we went. We uncovered anger at being sexualized in childhood–being denied the innocent exploration of sexuality that she might have had. She was angry at not being told about how her body works by her mother; that her early "boyfriends" knew more about her own body than she did. Underneath anger was fear that she might never really be the owner of her own body.

Now, when shame comes up, Amanda notices, accepts, releases, and asks Spirit for clarity about its origin. Sometimes the original conditioning comes to her mind (the abuse from her uncle), and sometimes it doesn't. If it does, it can provide additional clues as to the reasons for her behavior. If it doesn't, she still feels lighter and clearer. And she is now the person who is most intimate with her own body, as we all can be.

When we make an effort to consciously notice our emotions we have a better chance of (consciously) controlling our behaviors rather than have our emotions (unconsciously) control them.

I've described some more examples below of the intense emotions connected to abuse, and the possible effects on body and behavior. You will have your own, similar and different.

Anger

When I was a child, I felt angry over and over and over and over again. Every day, all the time.

"Oh, she's so well behaved!" my mother's friends would say— while inside my mind, I was screaming and yelling and wanting to kill someone. But I didn't. I was a very good little girl. I knew that my mother liked me more when I didn't complain or ask for her attention.

The cells with receptors for my anger neuropeptides were stimulated so often that the receptors for joy were barely used, so they would have mostly died off. I was more apt to feel anger and less apt to feel joy as I grew older.

If you repressed anger all your life and now have ulcers, it may not be your stomach. It may be your unexpressed anger. Have you ever gone out on a Friday night looking to feed your anger receptors?

One of my clients, Tamika, has experienced stomach sensitivity most of her life; she has experimented with eliminating different foods and had some relief; and now she is practicing letting her anger flow and finding more relief.

Up until our work together, she would judge herself harshly if she ever had a thought like, "I want to smash his face in." Well, that's an understandable thought toward someone who has abused you! I advise not actually trying to smash anyone's face in. I do advise expressing it in other ways–drawing, writing, dancing, yelling, talking, praying, climbing a mountain; skateboarding; surfing; anything that is not harmful to yourself or others.

Tamika practiced letting any anger she felt arise and flow through her. It was uncomfortable in the moment, but she felt noticeably lighter as the weeks went by. She chose time alone in the evenings for a while. She painted. She chose books and movies that she wanted to read and watch, not what she thought she should watch, or would be good for her to read. She observed and experienced her emotional landscape in private and didn't have to worry about or adjust to anyone else's opinions of her. This gave her more confidence–she knew herself better. And she was no longer afraid of any of her emotions.

Shame

I want to talk a bit more about shame because shame after abuse seems to be ubiquitous. It's my belief that we take on the shame of being abused because it is a way to pretend we are in control. The world just feels too dangerous if the abuse weren't our fault. Every time an abuse happens again, we decide to think it is our fault, or we are told it is our fault (because no one else wants to believe that Uncle Frank or Pastor Graham or Dad could have done that on his own, either). If we talk about our experience and place the blame where it belongs, it makes everyone uncomfortable; it makes others feel afraid or crazy or out of control.

If you felt aroused when you were abused, like I did, shame is probably an old friend of yours. Just because your body was aroused does not mean you invited the abuse.

For shame, the hypothalamus produces a major stress hormone that then causes an additional stress hormone to be released from the pituitary gland. The overall effect is believed to inhibit willpower, cloud thinking, and cause sluggishness in the body. So I'm never surprised when clients feel more buoyant as we peel back shame.

There is a very important piece to overcoming shame. It is a loving, non-predatory gaze. I did this with Tamika as we conducted our sessions via video conference. I can do this with you, too, or you can find someone you feel very comfortable with. They don't even have to know what you are doing. Just practice looking them in the eyes when you speak to them. Find someone who does not scare you, who does not want anything from you, and have a conversation with them. Look them in the eyes. Do not look away or down after each sentence. Keep practicing. Accept the discomfort.

I do this with every client. I look at each person in their Spirithood. I look into their eyes and see a Spirit inside a human body. This is the essence of Spiritualism. I see a Spirit worthy of dignity, respect, and Love. Over time, timidity ebbs away and in its place comes confidence.

Anxiety

My anxiety took the form of a constant feeling of butterflies in my belly. Actually, butterfly knives is a better description.

I never wanted to leave my mother's side. I was terrified of the world–even though my mother did not protect me well, she was all I had for a long time. As is typical for abused kids, I didn't "attach" properly to my parents–it's difficult to attach to people who do not have your best interests at heart –so I was not confident in being away from home. I wailed for weeks when I first started kindergarten.

But I discovered reading, and I then used that to distract myself from my feelings of fear and terror. I was desperate to learn to read properly so I could delve ever deeper into descriptions of places far away from where I was. I was desperate to read so I could learn everything about everything and maybe learn to protect myself somehow. I was desperate to read so I could imagine that someone in those stories loved me.

I used this method of distancing myself from my emotions all the way through high school. I studied every night for hours and hours. My mother once accused me of being addicted to reading and yelled at me to stop.

Little did I know, however, that the entire lining of the intestines, from the esophagus to the large intestine, including the cells of the seven sphincters, is lined with cells that contain neuropeptides and receptors: My feelings of insecurity and fear; my feelings of powerlessness and vulnerability and loneliness–my crippling anxiety–were right there with me all the time, in my gut.

The more often I did not express it, the larger it grew in my body. So, whenever I came out of my reading reverie and I was alone and terrified, my feelings of anxiety returned with a vengeance.

For example, I would cry when I had to interact with a new group of kids. This meant that I would want my mom to come get me from every birthday party and every sleepover when I was a child. I refused to have a babysitter. My mother detested this, as it was embarrassing for her and she couldn't get away from me.

As I got older, I started hyperventilating when I had to stand up for myself for any reason (like a job review). In these instances, rather than having a reasonable and manageable reaction, like other people might, I would have a huge reaction that was disproportionate to the situation. It really interfered with my employability.

All those years of trying not to feel these freaky emotions, trying not to recall these uncomfortable memories, had built up in my body to really toxic levels. My body couldn't hold any more. As a result of living in fight or flight for so long, I developed adrenal fatigue and, in my late 30s, spent years recovering. Chronic immersion in negativity is hazardous to health.

Overeating, Overdrinking, and Suicide

Neuropeptide Y (NPY) is the most abundant neuropeptide in the brain. Investigators have discovered that the hypothalamus secretes neuropeptide Y during emotional stress and has a calming effect. So, NPY helps us feel the emotional stress less acutely. (Variations in the genetic code for NPY produce variations in resilience to emotional trauma and stress, so it helps some of us more than others.)

NPY uses a receptor called Y1 to communicate with our cells about certain things. When NPY arrives and binds to Y1, it causes a cascade of biochemical events.

One of the effects is that some of the body's immune cells are prevented from working. This helps explain why we are more likely to get sick when under emotional stress. NPY also sends a message to our mind to eat. So, when we are stressed, our body releases more NPY and we feel like eating. This explains those movie scenes where we see a woman eating chocolate ice cream on the couch in her pajamas when her boyfriend dumps her.

Abuse causes emotional stress; NPY arrives, helps us calm down and also might make us sicker and want to eat more.

Studies have also shown that rats with fewer NPY receptors (Y1 and Y2) tend to consume a greater amount of alcohol and are less sensitive to the effects of alcohol. So, if we produce lots of NPY but it can't talk to our cells, we may want to drink more.

Studies have also shown that patients who have repeatedly attempted suicide have the lowest amount of NPY. So if our body tries to produce NPY under emotional stress but doesn't make very much (because of our specific DNA), we may feel more depressed.

Me, I was very, very, very depressed. I wanted to go to a counselor, but my parents wouldn't let me. "What are you going to tell them?" they asked. So, no talking about my emotional stress for me!

I also drank a whole lot from the age of 15 to the age of 30. My first drink was vodka. It was a balm; a salve; a holy experience. Suddenly, all the butterfly knives in my belly were gone. It was amazing and beautiful. After that first taste, I drank as much as I could as often as I could.

Drinking was a quick, easy, and very, very effective way of smothering my emotions, or "drowning my sorrows." But those emotions didn't die; they just stopped talking to me. Drinking my feelings worked extremely well through the end of high school and the beginning of college, but as the years went by, it interfered more and more with my ability to concentrate, read, get anywhere on time, protect myself from danger, and so many more things. Eventually, it hurt me more than it helped, and I got some help to stop. That help included talking a lot about my feelings.

I also suffered from PTSD pretty badly. I still have a hair-trigger startle response. For that, medication works well for me, along with more talk therapy. And I did try suicide (first at the age of about six and then again, sort of, at the age of 15). At six, I put a blanket over my head, sprayed whole cans of whatever aerosols I could find, and sealed the bottom of the door with a towel.

So, putting this all together, I wonder if I am one who produces less NPY or who has fewer Y receptors. It's an interesting thing to think about, but it doesn't really matter; what matters is that I did my damnedest to hide my emotional stress for years upon years upon years. And all that stress built up and had some toxic physical and behavioral effects.

Now I deal with emotional stress differently. Some things that work well for me are meditation, going to church, taking a walk, and listening to didgeridoo music (this really calms me down and reminds me of the Australian landscape, which was always comforting to me). None of these things distract me from my emotional stress; they help it flow through me. I accept it, and I let it flow through me. Sometimes I cry at church, and sometimes I fall asleep meditating. It's all good. Just keep those peptides flowing!

Sex and Relationships

It seems like common knowledge that those who were sexually abused behave promiscuously. I certainly did. And so did most of my clients. I think it's obvious that we were conditioned to believe that sexual attention equaled love. So, we go out and have sex. Sex does not equal love, though it can accompany love. Behaving as if they are one and the same does not lead to happiness. It leads to confusion and frustration and anger.

Similarly, we get ourselves into relationships that make us feel what we felt when growing up abused. We are chasing those neuropeptides to feed our receptors. Even though we may have consciously realized that we are making bad choices, we can't seem to stop. Shame comes into play again here. Shame tends to lead us into more abusive relationships, because we believe we must obey others to be loved.

For example, at age 27 or so, I got engaged. I felt panicked because he was showing signs of being very controlling. He was contemptuous in a humorous, subtle way. But I didn't trust myself to be sure. And those neurons were firing in a very familiar way. It felt just as right as it did wrong. I did marry him, and he was abusive. I left him when he tried to push me down some stairs.

At 32 or so, I found myself in another relationship with a man who was not so obviously abusive. This one spent my money and threatened suicide. He was, somehow, an abusive victim. I left him for the sake of our kids. I was fat and tired and

I knew that if I didn't leave, I wouldn't be able to save my health and be a good mother to the two children we had together.

After these relationships, I spent a few years trying to figure out what actually made me happy as regards sex and romance. Those adventures are a whole other book! I'm happy to say I did figure it out, and my partner is someone who is nothing like my father or my mother. He doesn't (often) trigger the same emotions they did. And when he does, I look at the origin of the feelings rather than blame him.

Mind in Matter

I'm not a neurobiologist (although I did take one summer school class in neurobiology at Harvard, for which I am proud to say I received a B), and the details of the peptide cascades and effects are much more detailed and nuanced than I understand or can describe here.

The point, however, is that repressing emotions is toxic. Repressing emotions is toxic because it causes blockages in the flow of peptides, which are the molecules of our emotions. The blockage upsets the balance in our bodies, and we suffer the consequences of physical symptoms and destructive behaviors.

All of this is not the old idea of mind over matter, it is mind in matter. Mind is body. Body and mind are one. Your subconscious mind is your body. The body is the physical manifestation of the mind. So, we can learn, with practice, to consciously control our reactions to stimuli, like the triggers that were installed by our trauma. We can retrain our minds and improve our bodies, our behaviors, our lives.

REFLECTION

- What are your main feelings about the abuse? (for example, hatred, sadness, resentment, smugness)

- How did your abusers and their accomplices convince you to keep quiet? (for example, by saying daddy will go to jail; by giving you treats; by looking at you in a certain way)

- What were (or are) the main effects on your body of not expressing your emotions about the abuse? (for example, chest pain, stomach ulcers, poor eyesight)

- What were (or are) the main effects on your behavior of not expressing your emotions about the abuse? (for example, stuttering; lying about other things; avoiding sex; unsafe sex)

- What were (or are) your medicines of choice? (for example, cutting, alcohol, sugar, work, tattoos)

- How did they (or do they) help you? (for example, alcohol sent me into sweet oblivion) How did they (or do they) harm you? (for example, alcohol stopped me from doing well in college)

- What are you feeling right at this moment? (for example, fear at what you are uncovering; contempt for me for daring to give advice; joy at the possibility of healing)

Chapter 3:
Twisted Thoughts

"Neurons that Fire Together, Wire Together!"

In the simplest of terms, neurobiologists and neuropsychologists like to explain things this way: when brain cells communicate frequently, the connection between them strengthens. Messages that travel the same pathway in the brain over and over begin to transmit faster and faster. Eventually we can go on automatic pilot.

This can be good with things like driving and hitting a golf ball. But, as we saw in Chapter 2, it can be detrimental when it comes to other behaviors, like seeking out relationships. We seek out situations that conditioned us as children; experiences that are similar to the instances of abuse that made our neurons wire together, that feed our neuropeptide receptors.

And so, the world feels dangerous. For us, it is. And people seem to be assholes. For us, they are. And men all seem to be bastards. For me, they were.

And we blame everything and everyone for our unhappiness. But our own thoughts have created our reality.

Choosing a Patsy

Some of my favorite things to blame for my unhappiness were the Catholic church (not that I was Catholic), the financial system, the human resources departments of various places, the police, several elementary school teachers, several of my friends' fathers (and mothers), and the staff of various visa offices around the world. But my very favorite was patriarchy.

For me, patriarchy was a perfect patsy–amorphous and unbeatable. I was the victim of patriarchy, and I was furious.

I couldn't get a good job because I was the victim of patriarchy (my father and the men who followed who had robbed me of my autonomy, my confidence, my very personhood). A good boyfriend was impossible to find because of patriarchy (all societal norms favored men and women could never be happy in a relationship). My high school science teacher had hugged me inappropriately, likewise other girls. One of my friend's boyfriends had raped her. Another friend had been raped by her friend's brother's friend at a sleepover. My dad had used me as bait for his business dealings. Past boyfriends had slapped me (patriarchy let them all get away with it). And of course there were more. So many more. I had gotten a reputation as a slut (patriarchy let the boys be studs). My mother had insisted I learn makeup and deportment so I could catch a man if I had turned out dumb (patriarchy meant boys didn't have to waste precious studying and reading time on learning to be ornamental; they could learn to be leaders). On and on and on.

But patriarchy alone was not the reason I was unhappy. My subconscious had me seeking out situations that fed my abundant neuropeptide receptors—my receptors for anger, anxiety, sorrow, and shame. My subconscious did not have me seeking out situations that fed my absent neuropeptide receptors—the receptors for joy and optimism and kindness. So, my conscious experience of the world was bleak. And I held the world responsible.

Choosing Responsibility

Yes, all these people are to blame. Patriarchy exists, and the individuals who perpetuate it are to blame for their actions.

They are to blame for participating in the oppressive patriarchal system. They are to blame for a lot of damage to me and to others.

They are responsible for their actions. But they are not responsible for my unhappiness. They are not responsible for my happiness. For that, I am responsible.

My blaming people and institutions for my unhappiness was a way of avoiding more emotional pain. If I could hold someone or something else responsible for my unhappiness, I was less afraid, because I was able to avoid the terrifying emotional unknown that I would have to explore were I to try to be happy. I did not know how to be happy. I did not know if I could ever be happy. It would be devastating to discover that, in fact, I could not be happy, even if I tried. Eventually, though, if I was to be happy, I would have to take responsibility for it myself.

Choosing Happiness

By blaming other people and institutions for my unhappiness, I was able to refuse to be humble or respectful; I was able to stay righteously angry, which is so deliciously enjoyable. But there comes a time when the pain hurts more than the cure. I was beaten; I surrendered to choosing happiness. I invite you to choose happiness, too.

REFLECTION

- Who is responsible for damage to your psyche and your soul and your body?

- Do you still blame them for your unhappiness?

- Do you blame anyone or anything else for your happiness?

- If I give you the tools, are you willing to pick them up and use them to bring yourself happiness?

Chapter 4:
There Is
A Reason for This

Love

    The ultimate purpose of life is to learn how to Love. That is, to learn how to turn irrational, erratic emotions into something purer and more refined and more useful. That something is Love. We can then generate more Love.

    Generating, being, accepting, and allowing Love to flow heightens our own spiritual vibration and allows us to access more knowledge of Spirit and continue to evolve. We feel more serene; we feel happier. Those around us feel it, too.

I wish there were a different word I could use than love. The word, love, has been used as an excuse to harm so many of us.

"Your father loves you, Steph."

"I love you so I want to make you into a better person"

Neither of these are Love. And I am sure you have examples of your own.

That's not to say that love such as a child's love, marital love, or parental love are not good and positive. They are. These are all different facets of Love.

I've heard the kind of Love I am talking about called "super love" and "unconditional love" and "pure love" and "God love" and "Christ consciousness." All of these are good terms. I sometimes use the terms Whole Love or Perfect Love.

It doesn't matter what we call it. It's just important to understand that it is love, given freely, without expectation of anything in return (like sex, or silence, or a lie, or a good test score, or having a baby, or baking a cake). It is not the same as romantic longing, or lust, or affection for a hat or for chocolate or for wine, or a crush on a celebrity.

We can feel Love flowing through us, but Love, itself, it is not a feeling. Love is the very stuff of the Universe. The more we make of it, the higher we rise and the happier we are.

To do that, we must learn to discern between Love and what many humans label "love." When we can recognize Love, we can choose Love and reject everything else with grace.

Discerning Pure Love from "Not-Love"

My parents did not Love me. They think they did. They say they did. But they did not. They used the word "love" to describe a feeling they had that, for them, justified any and every action. I think that feeling they described as love was yearning—yearning for Whole Love, Pure Love, Universal Love.

Their actions, then, were not coming from Love, but coming from their yearning for Love and their Fear of not having it. The way I understand it from my experience living with them is that their actions were coming from fear of aloneness. My father wanted to possess me and control me so as not to feel alone in this world. My mother chose my father over me to ensure he did not leave her alone in a culture that oppressed single mothers. She did not keep me safe; she did not choose me.

I learned from my parents. I chose relationships in friends and lovers that emulated my parents' relationships with me. Because this is what I understood to be Love. This was my model. These abusive behaviors were imprinted in my mind under the label "love." As every medical student learns, "neurons that fire together, wire together." So, my mind and body craved abuse and interpreted it as Love.

It makes perfect sense that the man I chose as my first husband sought to control and direct my actions like my father, and that the man I chose as my second husband withdrew from me, choosing himself and not me; giving me nothing; keeping love to himself; taking all I had and exhausting me, like my mother.

Moments of Joy

There were good things, too, in these relationships. My first husband was so funny; he brought me a lot of joy and that was real, and healing. It probably kept me there longer than necessary because it healed the wounds he made, but still, it was genuine happiness for those moments. My second husband was by my side physically, most of the time. When our children were born, he took care of them, and this meant I had time and space to recover. It also made me feel less alone, until it just wasn't enough to make up for his lack of spiritual presence.

As I said in Chapter 4, we ought not to hate our DNA, or we will hate ourselves. Similarly, we ought not to hate every one of our relationships. If we do, we risk not trusting ourselves in the future. We can recognize the joy, and we can recognize the abuse. We are complex, nuanced Spirit beings.

Earth School

What is special about Earth is that here, unlike in the Spirit realm, we have physical bodies and irrational emotions. On Earth, there is the full range of physical and spiritual senses to play with.

Physical pain and emotional pain are great teachers. When we are in enough pain, we choose to change, and we then have the opportunity to grow spiritually.

I often hear myself say, "Oh great, here's another damned opportunity for Spiritual growth."

We are Spirit first. We come to Earth School to test ourselves; to see if we can apply lessons learned before and to see if we have truly overcome weaknesses. Here we can learn for sure whether we have really evolved spiritually.

Planning

Learning Love is the ultimate goal, and there are infinite ways to learn it. Before we are born on Earth, in a human baby-body, we plan, in a general way, the shape of our life-to-come. We don't deal with many details, but we do plan our relationships to other humans and the kinds of situations we will encounter. This is in order to test our specific spiritual ideals on the way to learning perfect Love.

We want to test our spiritual ideals to see if they are real; to see if they are getting us closer to Love. If a soul has a spiritual ideal and desires to know if it actually possesses that ideal, the soul can come to Earth to test it. Only by becoming subject to the physical influences of the flesh and the laws of this physical realm can a soul know for certain if they really possess the spiritual ideal they seek.

We plan our Earth lives with our Spirit teachers. We have significant freedom to choose our earthly experiences, depending on the level of our current spiritual development. Some people decide to be born into easy conditions, and some people decide to be born into difficult conditions. Earth School also includes the opportunity to pay and receive karmic debts from our spiritual family: We can include experiences and situations in order to satisfy divine justice. A lot is planned, but many details are left up to free will and the great adventure we know as life.

We forget this planning when we come down to Earth because we need to be able to make decisions out of free will without being completely influenced by our higher knowledge. Any other way would be equivalent to a student being given the answers before taking a test. It is not a good way to learn.

Forgetting

I remember being in the womb. I remember floating in and out of my baby-body near the time of my birth into Earth School; floating into Spirit and back into Body. I remember kicking when I wanted my mother to move around so I could enjoy the rocking and go to sleep. I remember coming down the birth canal–not getting oxygen when I was moving, and then getting oxygen when I was not. I thought, "Wow, this is some adventure!" When I was born, I was born with my eyes open. The nurses squealed, "She has her eyes open!" When I saw the world (the hospital room) I thought, "I made this!" And there was my human ego coming into play! Pretty soon I forgot that I was part of Universal Love. Just as we are supposed to. And pretty soon I felt utterly alone, just as I was supposed to. I had to learn my lesson of empathy the hard way. Just as you have chosen to learn your lesson the hard way.

Remembering

Just because I forgot I was part of Universal Love, doesn't mean I ceased to be part of Universal Love. Just because I felt alone, doesn't mean I was alone. The trick is to remember. If we look around, if we listen carefully, we can see evidence of Universal Love and evidence of Spirit helpers who live in Love and who are always with us. And once we know we are not alone and always in Love, we can find the courage to walk away from abuse. So let's do it.

Why?

So, why do children suffer? Why do good people suffer? Why did this happen to you? It happened because you decided to learn this specific lesson on the way to the ultimate goal of learning Love.

You decided to learn it quickly and completely; that's why you chose to come to Earth School. And it also happened to you because you wanted to help other souls: We are spirit beings having a human experience and when we return to Spirit, everyone benefits from our human experience.

My Lesson

My specific lesson was empathy. My soul was holding onto pride, and judgment of others. I know this because, looking back, I realize that when I did not show empathy and kindness, I experienced the most emotional pain. I felt separate and isolated from whomever I was being nasty to, and that became unbearable.

By going through the terrible experience of abuse that I did, and behaving badly as a consequence (to others and to myself), I learned why other people might behave badly. I learned that any person who is selfish or cruel or a thief or a drunk or an addict or unclean or screaming at her kids or dirty or dishonest may have been damaged; may be trying to be good, but just is not able to do the right things, right now. I learned that everyone could be walking around in confusion and spiritual pain. I learned that I am no more worthy or less worthy than anyone else.

When I was a child, I felt superior to a lot of people. I was very very smart. When other kids would say dumb things, I just couldn't believe it; I couldn't fathom how a person couldn't understand something that seemed so basic to me.

As I went into elementary school, I had a lot of control over myself. I could say "no" to cookies and chocolates. I said "no" to soda. I got myself up and dressed and ready for school (or even earlier for swimming training or rowing practice) every day, on time. I did all my homework, and I did it well. I learned good manners and used them.

And then, I couldn't keep it together anymore. All of that control had been a result of my willpower. I had great willpower. I was planning to "just say no" to cigarettes. It seemed easy when I was 12.

But by the time I was 15, I was exhausted and angry and resentful, and I was more and more anxious. Being good had not given me entry to the enchanted kingdom I had thought was my due.

So, I had a cigarette. I coughed and spluttered, but I liked the feeling of damage it gave me: the feeling of burning myself from the inside out. And it gave me a feeling that I could focus on instead of my growing anxiety and anger and resentment. I could focus on the burn.

My mother smoked every night as she sat in silence and watched TV while she sewed. I sat with her in the hope she would pay me some attention. She hardly ever did. One time, I asked her if I could have one. I didn't even know what cigarettes were, but she obviously loved them (small L); she paid them more attention than she paid me. I thought perhaps if I had one, I could share in her activity and we would be closer. I was about eight, I think. She didn't give me one then, and she was horrified when she found out I had started smoking years later because I had been so arrogant and unforgiving about it. Even while smoking myself, I had kept at her and at her until she eventually quit, went into nicotine withdrawal, and spewed blood and black gunk into the kitchen sink.

I also had a drink–knowingly and deliberately. I had had alcohol as a kid–my sister had given me fruity wine, my parents had let me have Irish coffee, that sort of thing–but after this drink, I didn't stop. This drink, at 15, was the cure for anger and anxiety and resentment. The moment before I had that slug of vodka, I didn't understand what alcohol was or could do. The moment after that slug of vodka, the butterflies with knives in my belly were drowned. They were silent. And so I kept drinking. That night and as many nights after that as I could.

Pretty soon, my grades started falling. And then I started forgetting high school obligations, like sports events. Once I started college, I stopped studying properly for exams. I lied to professors about why I wasn't getting assignments done on time. I tried to be honest and kind with friends and boyfriends, and a lot of the time, I was. But a lot of the time, I wasn't. I ran away and travelled around the world for a time. For a little while, I begged and slept on the streets and stayed in a squat with a pack of dogs. People looked down on me, saying things like, "We don't want people like you around here." Twice, I was thrown down stairs. I went back home; I sold drugs; I considered becoming a whore because that was the only way I could think of to make enough money to support myself.

I had gone from superior to inferior.

But I was the same soul, the same spirit. I felt the same inside. I was the same inside. It was a rough way to learn that truth—that we are all the same inside; that we are all Spirit; that we are all equal.

This lesson of empathy and kindness didn't come as an epiphany. It came bit by bit. As a child, I knew in my bones that kindness was right (I guess I remembered it from being in Spirit), but I forgot as I grew (as I was meant to) and I had to test it out; I had to learn it viscerally, physically, emotionally. And I continue to test this spiritual principle that we are all equally worthy of love and kindness. When I treat others with love and kindness, I am happier; happier in a deep and satisfying way, even if it is more comfortable and more thrilling to play around in feelings like righteous anger and arrogance for a while.

[You Don't Have to] Love Your Enemy

So, if everyone is equal, if everyone is worthy of love and kindness, that means my abusers are, too, right? Well, yes.

And here is where most people say you should forgive. Forgive! Understand they are human, too. Have compassion. They are suffering. Don't hold a grudge; don't hold it against them. As if it's our responsibility to make the abuser feel OK. As if they are the victim.

They are not the victim, and we have no responsibility for their well-being.

Trauma, by definition, is the result of exposure to an inescapably stressful event (or pattern of events) that overwhelms a person's coping mechanisms. So, enough with having us protect our abusers; we are overwhelmed enough.

Our abusers are worthy of love, yes. But we don't have to do it. It is not our responsibility. Spirit can take care of that. You can call it God or whatever you like. I call it Infinite Intelligence.

The only thing we have to do to be happy is to take responsibility for our own happiness. Does it make you happy to sit and try to understand your abuser's point of view? Their terrible childhood? Their fears and disadvantages? It might. But then, you probably wouldn't be reading this book.

You may choose to confront your abusers. I did. I called my father every curse word I could think of. It made me feel better, but not much. My dad sat there weeping crocodile tears and denying it all and blaming me for ripping the family apart. I hated him all the more.

One of my clients confronted her mother, and her mother said she remembered nothing of the abuse. She admitted it might have happened, but claimed that she remembered none of it. Other clients have considered a confrontation, but have decided against it. It is certainly not a prerequisite to happiness and usually does not change much. If we pin our happiness onto some kind of confrontation or admission of guilt we are still in thrall to our abuser; they still have power over us.

You may eventually get to the point of accepting and understanding and loving your abusers; the great spiritual masters are capable of that. But it is not a prerequisite to happiness, and it is not your job. So just forget about trying. As you find ways to make yourself happier, it will come naturally. You will find yourself thinking about the abuser suddenly one day, and feel less hatred, less anger; less everything. So do not burden yourself for one more second with that definition of forgiveness.

[You Do Have to] Love Your DNA

I will say, though, that there is one very important thing to do if you were abused by a family member. You must find something about them that you admire. Your family is your DNA. If you hate everything about them, you will hate your own DNA; you will hate yourself; you will catch sight of yourself in the mirror looking like your brother and want to smash your own face; or you will feel an urge to paint, like your mother, and avoid it even though you really enjoy it.

In my case, my father was a good provider; he provided a high-quality lifestyle for me, my mother, my sisters, and some other family members. We had good food, a nice house, vacations; lovely clothes; a good education. I do the same for my family. I admire it in myself, and I learned it from him.

My mother is a very talented seamstress and has a very highly developed fashion sense. I have always enjoyed dressing well and looking stylish. Even when I was living in rags, they were good-looking rags that complemented my dreadlocks.

REFLECTION

- What is the most burning moral truth you feel? What makes you cry or shout when you see a movie about it? (for example, is it kindness, generosity, equality, courage, fortitude?)

- In what moments do you feel happy? (for example, when you help a sick animal; when you give money away without anyone knowing; when you play piano)

- Do these two things have anything in common? (this is the key to the lesson you chose for yourself; this lesson is your doorway to Perfect Love and happiness)

Chapter 5:
You Are Not Alone

I don't remember much of Spirit and Love throughout my childhood, but there were moments when it came shining through.

Like when my great aunt would read me stories. Many weekends, my mother would send me to her mother's place to stay. My grandmother, my grandmother's husband, and my grandmother's sister lived there. I remember hearing my mom on the phone saying, "Mom, I can't handle her." I wasn't badly behaved, but I did ask my mother for attention; I did ask her to play with me and I did ask her if we could go places together. I guess it was just my existence she couldn't handle.

Anyway, there was one story called *Monty the Runaway Mouse*. He ran away and was looking for a new mother because he felt his own did not love him. He tried a big soft doll–he whispered in her ear, but she did not answer; he tried a birds' nest, but he was thrown out; he tried a soft cuddly ginger cat, but she wanted to eat him. Eventually he went back home, where his mother cooked him good food and took care of him. For me, that was the saddest ending I could imagine.

My great aunt saw my sorrow and nudged me and whispered, "Do you want to find a new mother?" I said nothing in return, but in that moment I knew there must be a Love truer and healthier than what I had at home. I could feel it.

There was another moment when one of my mother's acquaintances came to the house. They were having the conventional conversation about kids. I was about four.

The woman asked me, "Are you looking forward to starting school?"

I replied, "What's school?" She laughed and looked at me as if I were the cutest thing.

I said, "Mommy, what's school?" The woman looked horrified.

My mother said, "I haven't talked to her about it yet."

She asked, "What are you doing today? Are you going to play with some kids?"

I said, "There are other kids?" The woman looked even more horrified. And angry now.

I hadn't known that other kids even existed. I suppose I must have seen them in the supermarket or something, but I had never been taken to play with any.

My mother said to her, "Oh, there aren't really any other kids around here."

The woman said, "I will be back to see you." She looked right at me. I felt seen. I felt connected. But I didn't see her again. I suppose my mother didn't invite her in the next time.

In these moments, I understood that there was something good and healthy connecting me to other people; something that felt like a flowing river; something that allowed us to communicate without words. And so it continued: When I was about nine, I sensed the night my great aunt would die. I was not surprised, I was not angry; I knew she was happy to go although maybe a bit annoyed that I had taken up a lot of her time at the dinner table the evening before with making her guess riddles.

Once, in my early 20s, I was spending an evening with a friend, having dinner and martinis. Suddenly we heard water rushing in the chimney, and then a bell–loud and clear and pure.

I felt uplifted; I wasn't scared at all. Surprised, yes, but not afraid. It was lovely.

There were other times when I would be having a conversation with a friend and I would say something like, "Oh but you're going to live in London, anyway," or, "Oh, don't worry, the next man you meet will be the one."

My friends would say, "But how do you know? Why do you sound so sure?"

"I don't know," I would reply. It just felt true.

In my late 20s, I was traveling through Costa Rica on my way to my new life in New York City. I was sitting on the hotel bed with my boyfriend. We had just arrived. Suddenly, the bed started shaking. My boyfriend was scared; I was more like thrilled. Then water started pouring out of the faucet, rushing out. I went into the bathroom, and the tap was not open. I opened it and then closed it. The water stopped. The bed stopped. I started laughing. I felt relief wash over me; I suddenly felt really happy that I was not alone on Earth. Here was evidence that there were other entities interested in me, wanting to communicate with me, wanting to somehow be in my life.

Evidence of Spirit People

As I approached 30, I started reading literature about and by the great spiritual masters, and I went to a class to enhance my intuition. I was smart, but I had not been able to analyze my way into happiness. I had finally realized that I had to go about it a different way. I know I can't analyze my way into happiness, but I did find the doorway to happiness like that, and at every step, I check the validity of what I find.

During my time taking that class, I saw irrefutable evidence of the spirit world. I attended spirit circles during which I received messages from my grandparents, spirit guides, relatives, and friends through the mediums who were also present. I also received messages in my dreams. I learned to meditate in a way that worked for me, and I began to feel much calmer.

Some of the messages I received included advice to take salt baths, go on a retreat I was thinking of, meditate on a white flower to help with a decision, spend money on myself rather than to impress others, rent the beach house for my kids. One of my favorites (from my grandfather) was, "Take heart, if your great uncle and I could survive the New Guinea jungle in World War II, you can survive your divorce." Old boyfriends in Spirit came to tell me they were sorry. Old friends came to tell me I had helped them through a tough time. I took their advice, I opened my mind to their ministering, and I became happier.

Then, a few years later, my father was on his deathbed. I told my mother I would come down to Australia to say goodbye to him. I hadn't spoken to him in 15 years or so. She told my father that I was coming. The next day, my father died. At the moment of his death, I felt him. A happiness came over me as I felt him checking up on me at work in my office in Manhattan. My phone rang just then. It was my sister telling me he had passed. Suddenly, his earthly personality was gone and I was relieved. I was happy he was dead.

I was hoping that would be it. I was hoping he would just go off and live happily ever after in Spirit. But no. He came through a medium to speak to me. I said, "I do not want to hear from that man. Tell him to go away." And he did. The medium did tell me, though, that he was on the other side, a bit surprised to be there, but learning about how to get along.

I went down to Australia to the funeral. My sister blamed me for tearing the family apart, as did her son. But I had no fear; I had the Love of Spirit with me. I shed some tears of grief and sorrow for not having a loving family, and I let the emotions flow through me, I told the truth about my feelings to those I could trust not to try to hurt me, and I was serene.

We get along much better, now, my father and I. He came through another medium friend of mine. She described his defining physical characteristics precisely, the family tree, and so on, so I knew it was him. Then she said, "He has three things to say: I am not who I thought I was. I was not a good father. I'm sorry."

And finally, I had my apology. The thing I had been wanting my whole life. He wasn't capable of doing it here on Earth. But the door to reformation is never closed. He was capable of it in Spirit.

Getting that apology was slightly satisfying. I felt a bit of righteousness. And I felt that final bit of self-doubt leave me. But it was certainly not the key to happiness. The key to happiness was spiritual growth.

REFLECTION

- What actions did your abuser(s) label "LOVE"?

- What feeling(s) were you afraid of experiencing if you rejected the abuse?

- What moments of happiness did you have with your abusers?

- What evidence do you have of Love? (What did it feel like?)

- What evidence do you have of Spirit? (What did it feel like?)

- What evidence do you have of Spirit beings? (What did it feel like?)

- With the Love of your Spirit helpers, will you walk away from abuse?

Chapter 6:
The Art of Forgiveness –
3 As

Once you have learned to trust your instincts, express your emotions, and take responsibility for your actions (your happiness), you can do it again and again and again. Once you have found a reason for living, and experienced the safety and love of Spirit, you can call upon them again and again. Every time you do these things, you will feel more comfortable and go a bit deeper; you will grow in confidence and happiness and serenity and a world of joy will begin to open up, ever farther from the echoes of the abuse.

In this way, you will be peeling back the layers that the abuse has slathered on you. You will be sensing your essence. When you are living according to your essence, and not in reaction to the abuse and the abuser, you will find peace. This is the art of forgiveness.

Accept. Admit. Act.

I have composed a simple mnemonic that distills the art of forgiveness: Accept. Admit. Act. Accept the moment. Admit you are responsible for your own happiness. Act accordingly.

Accept the Moment

This really means that we accept the emotions we are having at this moment. Sometimes we have to sit still and hurt.

When we are feeling fine and easy we usually don't have to do anything about it, we are just doing life. But if we feel anxious, or something similar, we are more likely to notice. Anxiety and her sisters like nervousness, panic, and foreboding are usually us worrying about the future. If we feel depressed, or something similar, we are more likely to notice. Depression and her cronies like sorrow, grief, and despair are usually us worrying about the past.

So, when we feel anxious or depressed or any other variation of fear or anger, it's a good idea to just accept those feelings.

Accept the emotions, and let them flow through us (let the peptides flow!).

When we do this, we are actually entering the mind-body network with our conscious mind and playing a part in ensuring no blockages occur, which means that these emotions will be less likely to lodge in the body and cause harm. So, stay in the moment, accept the moment; accept your emotions, let the peptides flow!

Breathing is the key to acceptance. The peptide-respiratory link is well-documented. Virtually any peptide can be found in the respiratory center. This appears to explain the powerful calming and healing effects of consciously controlled breathing patterns. So, do breathe through your emotions. Observe your breathing whenever an uncomfortable emotion comes along and practice keeping it slow and steady.

Admit You Are Responsible for Your Own Happiness

When we live in accordance with the laws of nature, we are in harmony with ourselves and the Universe, so we feel peace and serenity. It is our choice whether or not to live in accordance with the laws of nature, or not. This is free will.

The laws of nature include things like the law of cause and effect. When we act out of Love, we receive Love. When we behave generously, we will receive in kind. The earthly existence is but a fragment of life. The consequences of deeds done on Earth stay with the soul when the body dies. The soul goes on and each soul must work out for itself a salvation. We are all subject to the immutable laws of nature and when we transgress them, we experience misery and loss; when we respect them, we secure advancement and satisfaction. There are no favorites and there is no unfair punishment for those who were unable to avoid error.

So don't worry that your abuser is getting away with anything. No action is free of consequence. They will, literally, get theirs. You may not see it here on Earth, but there is no escape.

Act Accordingly

I can give you the essentials, but you will have to find out what works. Take care of your body, your mind, and your soul. Take care of your Self.

For the body, go to the doctor and a dentist for a check-up if you haven't in a long while. Choose clothes that fit properly and are appropriate for the weather. Exercise, even if just a little, even if you are depressed. Keep your body and home clean. Get advice from experts if you are not sure of how to do these things effectively.

For the mind, consider therapy. Read books that hold your interest. Watch movies that hold your interest. Don't read or watch anything because you feel you should or because others are. Keep a journal if it makes you happy.

For the soul, find out what you love. Is it dancing? Take a class. Do you get a frisson of pleasure when you make yourself a nice sandwich? Perhaps take it further and learn about nutrition or gourmet cooking. Whenever you feel a spark or joy, follow it; whenever you see the end of a string of happiness, pull on it.

Prayer may be something you choose. It does not have to be formal. It does not even have to be in words. A spontaneous cry of the soul to Spirit is all that is needed. Spirit friends are always near, just a thought away. There are Spirit friends of every sort, for every need. Spirit friends are ever present and ever ready to take your message upward until it reaches a power that can respond. Listen, and you will hear them speaking to you in your dreams and your quiet moments.

Remember, though, that you may not receive the answer you expect. Sometimes, granting our requests would do us harm. But the prayer is always heard. And prayer is most effective when it is regular. Prayer will bring you closer to Spirit; you will feel less burdened by suffering.

Try not to be impatient. Spiritual growth is infinite. There is no end.

Summary

1. Accept the moment.

   In the moment: Accept your emotions; allow them to be there. Breathe.

   Long-term: Meditate; listen to the great teachers; cultivate mindfulness; do not wish for the past to be different or the future to be particular. Admit you are responsible for your own happiness.

2. Admit you are responsible for your own happiness.

   In the moment: Admit that you have a choice of actions. You can choose not to react to the emotion as you used to, not to inflict harm on yourself or someone else. Your emotions do not have to control you. Make a decision right now to act in your own best interests.

   Long-term: Admit that you are powerful. You can influence things in the real world. Make a list of when and how you have made yourself happier and your life better, even if in a small way, like hanging some beautiful curtains that filter the light in a comforting way, or getting a dog to love. As you take each action from now on, notice how your life gets better. When you falter and doubt yourself, look back at your successes for evidence.

3. Act accordingly.

   In the Moment: Ask your spirit helpers to guide you and comfort you. Take care of any immediate physical need like drinking some water, or getting some sleep, or removing yourself from a dangerous situation.

   Long-term: Consider therapy; treatment for any addictions; a medical checkup; notice what activities (other than overdrinking or overeating) put a smile on your face and joy in your heart. Do more of those.

Chapter 7:
The Nature of Reality

The illusion of separateness gives rise to fear and unhappiness. The feeling of being at the mercy of external events gives rise to fear, depression, and anxiety.

But when we know that we are connected to an infinite intelligence, that we are connected to individuals in Spirit who care for us and wish only the best for us, we need not feel lonely or scared. When we understand that all is unfolding exactly as it should, we can surrender to life as it unfolds.

But I do not expect you to have blind faith in these notions. Western science is beginning to be able to prove it using their methods. Modern physics now postulates that consciousness determines events. Nothing we experience happens without our influence. All of reality is entangled, and we affect it by being in it.

If you're interested, I have outlined the scientific discoveries below. The experiments are all with subatomic particles; the smallest parts of matter we can measure. This is quantum physics.

1920

Niels Bohr and Werner Heisenberg were the first to claim that before a measurement is made, a subatomic particle doesn't really exist in a certain place or have a certain motion. It isn't anywhere. Only when its wave function collapses does it become somewhere.

For many years, physicists thought that the wave function of a particle had to be collapsed by hitting a particle with a particle of light, or something. But it was later discovered that just the thought of the observer could collapse a particle's wave function and give it a definite position in space and time. Nothing is real until it is observed.

1926

Max Born demonstrated that quantum waves are waves of probability, not waves of material. Quantum waves are statistical predictions, that is, nothing but a likely outcome; nothing but a description of the likelihood of an event. Nothing happens until the event is observed. As John Wheeler said, "No phenomenon is a real phenomenon until it is an observed phenomenon."

1935

Albert Einstein, Boris Podolsky, and Nathan Rosen wrote about particle entanglement. Quantum theory predicted that a particle could somehow know what another particle far, far away was doing. Einstein dismissed this theory. He called this weirdness "spooky action at a distance," and he attributed it to some unknown contamination of the experiment. Einstein insisted that nothing could influence anything else at speeds above light speed.

But Einstein was wrong. Einstein's notion of space-time is just a mathematical tool that helps us explain the movement of objects. Space-time does not exist in the physical universe. We use the tool of space-time to measure objects in relation to each other. It's convenient for us at our level of evolution. But nothing is limited by space-time. In reality, separate events do not happen in separate locations. The presence of the observer is hopelessly entangled with whatever he or she is observing.

Eventually, Einstein admitted that "the distinction between past, present, and future is only a stubbornly persistent illusion."

1964

John Bell proposed an experiment that could show whether separate particles can influence each other at great distances. He finally destroyed the possibility of what some people call "local realism," that is, an objective, independent universe such as Einstein described. Before Bell, many still insisted that physical states exist before they are measured, that particles had definite attributes and values. They do not. Before matter can exist, it has to be observed by a living creature.

1982

The Aspect Experiment in France demonstrated that two once-connected quantum particles separated by vast distances remained somehow connected. If one particle was changed, the other changed–instantly. Scientists don't know the mechanics of how this faster-than-the-speed-of-light travel can happen, though some theorists suggest that this connection takes place via doorways into higher dimensions.

1997

Nicholas Gisin proved that particles communicate with one another instantaneously, not even delayed by the time light travels that far. In his experiment, it was seven miles. Gisin sent photons (bits of light) along separate optical fibers. One encountered interference, at which point it could take one of two paths. Gisin found that whatever option one photon took, its twin would take the other. Instantaneously. From seven miles away.

2002

David Wineland used beryllium ions in a similar experiment and proved that communication is instantaneous and wrote, "There is spooky action at a distance." The ions knew what would happen in the future.

2004

The famous double slit experiment took place. Probability waves of individual photons interfere with themselves. An electron is both a particle and a wave. Where the electron is located is dependent upon the act of observation. Everything we observe is floating in a field of mind. Erwin Schrodinger called it entanglement.

How This Helps

When feelings of loneliness, depression, and anxiety come visiting, Spirit friends seem far away, and you feel a bit crazy, it can be comforting to remember that science proves that we are certainly not alone in the universe. We are connected to an infinite intelligence that enables us to be the masters of our destiny; that allows us to be the authors of our own happiness.

Chapter 8:
Moving Forward

Freedom

Forgiveness is freedom from anger and resentment. Reaching this state has nothing to do with the perpetrator of the abuse. Certainly, the abusers' actions (there were probably more than one) led to your pain, and they will be held accountable, but not by you.

And if the abusers are subject to earthly justice, like jail, or losing their business, or even just embarrassment within the community, it will not suddenly make you free of anger and resentment. It may make you happy in some way, but it does not lead to forgiveness; it does not guarantee spiritual freedom for you.

Freedom from anger and resentment has everything to do with your choices moving forward. You can choose to accept things as they are, choose to accept that you are responsible for your happiness, and choose to act in accordance with that. Or you can choose not to. Forgiveness is an art, a spiritual process that you are in control of.

When I gave birth to my second child, I was able to deliver him without any painkillers and in a pretty short time. I had made a decision before the labor started that I would accept what was happening at each moment. I would go with the flow; feel the fear and do it anyway. I breathed into the pain, the fear, the instructions I was hearing; the grief at not having a loving mother with me; all of it. I breathed deeply and I did not hyperventilate: I did not resist the emotions. I consciously accepted each sensation and allowed it to flow through me. I did not resist. I breathed into everything.

Apparently, I was plugging into my periaqueductal gray (an area of the midbrain filled with opiate receptors, making it a control center for pain) and resetting my pain threshold. Not that I knew at the time precisely what was going on, or even the words "periaqueductal gray"! All I knew was that I was living in my body and mind at the same time.

However, with my first child, I did resist. I was afraid of what would happen to me, to the baby, to my marriage; I was angry at being fat and being without a loving family; I was stressed at people touching me; I was worried about money. And more.

That labor was more than 50 hours long and required painkillers, an epidural, and finally forceps! Perhaps if I had chosen to ACCEPT the fear and anger and all its variations flow through me and out again, and whatever came next (relief? hope? peace? more anger? eventually sleep!), ADMIT that I had a choice about being in pain, and ACTED accordingly, I may have had an easier time.

This may not sound like forgiveness of my abuser. But it is. By accepting my feelings, taking responsibility for my own happiness, and acting accordingly, I am happy. Do you see?

Forgiveness is not dependent on my father or his actions; his life or his death; or his apology or his admission of guilt. Forgiveness is freedom from anger and resentment. That is all.

Fatigue

You will get tired and slip back into blaming others for your unhappiness. I did it for years. And I have seen clients do it, especially those going through a divorce. It is so very easy to blame the ex-husband, or "men." There will be times when you feel that this process will never end; that life is just one big tangle of confusion and unfairness. It's easy to fall back into anger and resentment because they are comfortable, familiar, and justified. But hanging on to them will not lead to happiness. It will lead to spiritual dissatisfaction, restlessness, discontent, and then self-medicating with food or alcohol or sex or something else.

I've seen clients become refreshed after having attended a healing circle. When you're with others committed to spiritual growth, it is inspiring and comforting. My circles are not cognitive therapy groups, so there's no requirement to share personal details. We meditate a little, we connect with Spirit, and we receive healing energy and helpful messages from spirit friends.

One group member receives regular visits from her unborn child, now a little girl in spirit. The little girl loves her so much and is so proud of her mama. My client can now see this spirit child herself and always leaves in a serene and grateful frame of mind.

Doubt and Self-Pity

Fatigue may lead to losing faith. Or doubt may pop up on its own out of nowhere. The ideas I have presented here may be very new ideas for you.

One common thought is that of not deserving the abuse. This easily leads to a feeling of self-pity. Many people cannot easily accept that they had a hand in choosing such a difficult spiritual challenge, and doubt the reality that our souls survive the change we call death.

This is when communicating with Spirit through a medium really helps. It provides proof. Also, it just feels right and true. I have found it calms clients down and helps them practice trusting their instincts.

A client of mine, Catherine, had a mother who was not capable of loving her. The mother was anorexic, unemotional, and unconnected to her children. She didn't feed the children enough; she didn't keep a clean home or a safe home; she left feces on the floor in the bathroom; and didn't pay attention to her children's schooling. My client had to protect herself from the extraordinary sorrow of having a mother physically present, yet so absent. She protected herself by choosing (albeit unwittingly) not to feel. As an adult, my client has difficulty in actually recognizing her own emotions.

We contacted her mother in Spirit. Her mother showed herself to me as a very, very thin woman with her insides showing, raw and bleeding. I described this spirit person to my client, and she confirmed that it sounded like her mother, who was always demanding in one way or another that her issues be front and center, that she be the center of attention in her sickness and helplessness.

My client's mother communicated to her daughter, through me, that she was living happily enough on the other side and occasionally in contact with other family members who had crossed over. Her mother came through several times, over a series of weeks.

By serving as the medium between my client and her mother, and also speaking with my client's spirit guides, I was able to help my client understand the purpose of her having chosen this mother who could not love her.

My client had set herself a difficult challenge—that of testing the spiritual principle of accepting love. When she becomes brave enough to make herself vulnerable enough to risk the pain of rejection she will open herself to being loved. Then she will experience, viscerally, the result of accepting love: the happiness, the satisfaction, the knowledge that it is what life is all about. And her soul will never again doubt it.

Every time my client communicated with her mother in Spirit, she softened a little. She was able to cry a little more. That is, she was able to accept her emotions. She was able to tell her mother she loved her, and she was able to stop worrying so much about taking care of her mother. She was able to admit she was responsible for her own happiness. She is slowly finding that a more supple approach to relationships leads to spiritual resilience. That is, she is healing herself. This is the art of forgiveness.

Fear

Just beginning this process shows that you have the courage you need to complete it. But yes, fear may be a constant companion. I have observed that it is fear of the unknown. Often, fear prevents us from understanding ourselves.

As you continue to peel away the layers that have been covering your true essence, you will experience strong emotions, and they may not always be what you expect. You may also have new memories come up, or connect things in new ways.

At the time Amanda came to me for help, her boyfriend was stalking her; smashing her car and calling her work. She was frustrated at so often choosing abusive men.

Of course, the first order of business was to get her to a place where she could be clear-headed enough to make decisions in her interest; to act rather than react; to protect herself without disrupting her life further.

During our first session, Bernardo, a Capuchin Monk, came through in Spirit for her. He came to join her especially for this healing process. He told us that he would guide her thoughts so that she would not become so distraught and distracted by the fear of her abusive former boyfriend–thus enabling her to concentrate more fully on healing. He told us that he would also encourage her to put her feelings into words rather than suppress them and deny them. Bernardo really helped her feel safe and increased her trust in herself. He stayed with her throughout the process. We all have such loving spirits around us.

Pretty soon, she was able to make calm decisions about whether to leave or stay in her home; whom to trust with what was going on in her life; whether to make police reports, and so on.

As my client and I (and Bernardo) continued to work together, she told me about her grandfather, who had abused her mother. She had not known this until her mother, on her deathbed, confessed to her sister. Then my client found out through another family member. Together we put these clues together–she had always felt uncomfortable around her grandfather but had been told she should not feel that way. This helped her realize why she had not trusted her own instincts about men and chosen abusive relationships instead.

During subsequent sessions, a lovely, bubbly, joyful presence visited with us and infused the days that followed with optimism for my client. This presence didn't provide a name or show us a form, it was just energy to enlighten and heal. As we talked about the past and uncovered the thoughts and behaviors that had formerly protected her but were no longer helping her, her Spirit guides advised us about the present: she was to call on them as she worked (in her artistic field) and they would form a protective layer between her and the public so that she could remain emotionally open to her audience, but safe from any predatory forces.

She continues to use the tools I taught her and to ask Spirit for help. She is becoming the master of her own actions and the master of her happiness.

Chapter 9:
You Can Do It

By now you should understand that you were conditioned by one or more abusers and their accomplices not to trust your instincts (that little voice inside) and not to honor your emotions; you went on to ignore that little voice and squelch your emotions to please others, and this damaged your health and twisted your behavior. This is not your fault; it is just what happened.

Now that you understand all this, you can choose to act differently. You can blame your abusers as much as you like; they are most certainly responsible for their actions. And you are responsible for yours.

It's easier to choose to take responsibility for our actions, and therefore our happiness, when we understand that before we came to Earth (when we were in spirit), our soul chose this set of circumstances in partnership with our spirit teachers, to provide ourselves a spiritual challenge; to test a certain spiritual principle or principles; to evolve spiritually. This is your purpose on Earth.

And we are not alone. Our spirit guides are always just a thought away. The nature of reality is that we are all connected. We are all entangled. No one escapes divine justice; no one escapes divine love.

Remember the practical tool that helps to peel away the layers of distrust of yourself that your abusers pasted on you: Accept. Admit. Act.

My Wish for You

I just recently had this little revelation: I used to really hate having to go out to any kind of "event." The theater, a dinner party, a graduation ceremony—those kinds of things. Whenever I was invited, I had feelings of frustration and annoyance. My thoughts were that I must not like the person who invited me or, if that were clearly not true, then that I must be an introvert, or that I couldn't really afford the ticket. I instantly came up with all these kinds of intellectual rationales to explain my feelings.

But recently, I took my own advice when these feelings came up over a (free) concert I was invited to (with people I wanted to be with).

I just literally stood still for a few moments so I could ACCEPT the feeling of annoyance. I let it wash over me rather than resisting its effect and smothering it with thoughts. I just gave the feeling some space and time. And you know what? A sense memory surfaced. It was a memory (actually numerous images) of times when I attended these kinds of "dressy" events as a young woman. I was always cold. I was always hungry. So, I was always annoyed and frustrated!

I was always cold because I'd feel I had to wear something skimpy or clingy and include high heels–I felt obliged to wear something sexy. Of course, this was because that was how my mother dressed to please my father; having been sexually "activated' as a child, sexiness was how I thought one should be in the world to be valued as a woman. I was always hungry because I was staying thin for the same reasons.

So, these feelings of annoyance were connected to a pretty primal experience. An experience that had no relevance to the present moment.

Next, I ADMITTED that I was in control of my reaction to this invitation. I could go, or not go. I could choose to be annoyed or not. I chose not to be annoyed. And I chose to go.

So, I ACTED. The following week, I dressed warmly. I wore low-heeled boots and my favorite comfy coat. My clothes were in good repair and had some personality. My coat is by a French designer and I bought it in San Francisco visiting a good friend. It feels good to wear it.

And this, my friends, is forgiveness. My dad is to blame for abusing me. But he is not in control of my thoughts and feelings and behavior today. I am. It's not easy all the time, but it's true–I am in control of my thoughts and feelings and behavior. I am responsible for my actions today. Happiness is in my power. And in yours.

What to Do Next

Put into practice the 3 As: Accept. Admit. Act. Every day. Know that emotions cannot kill you if you let them flow. So let them flow. Know that there is an Infinite Intelligence of which you are a part; it is Pure Love. So let it in. Know that your abusers will not escape divine justice. They literally cannot get away with it.

As the days and weeks and months and years go by, you will feel lighter and more peaceful. One day you will realize that the abuse no longer echoes in your mind and your body. That is the day you will say you are over it. You will have forgiven.

It is on that day that you will understand, as Rumi said, that, "there is a secret medicine given only to those who hurt so hard they can't hope." That secret medicine is the complete and utter understanding of Grace. The experience of the infinite and infinitely loving power of Spirit.

Amen.

Further Reading

Spirit Teachings by William Stainton Moses

Molecules of Emotion: Why You Feel the Way You Feel by Candace B. Pert

Biocentrism: How Life and Consciousness are the Keys to Understanding the True Nature of the Universe by Robert Lanza and Bob Berman

Life in the World Unseen by Anthony Borgia

The Principles
Of Spiritualism

Spiritualism bows to no creeds or dogmas; it does not require blind faith in anything. Its philosophy is centered around principles which were received directly from Spirit in 1871 through the mediumship of Emma Hardinge Britten (1823–1899)[1,2].

The principles have evolved over time and you will find them expressed differently by different churches around the world. I present them here as expressed by the National Spiritualist Association of Churches (NSAC), one of the oldest and largest of the national Spiritualist church organizations in the United States.

These are principles, not commandments, and in accepting them, every person is allowed and encouraged complete liberty of interpretation based upon their experience and investigation.

I am an ordained Minister of the Gospel of Spiritualism, and what you find described in this book is my application of the principles to everyday life; it is an application and interpretation that I have found useful to me and others in the pursuit of happiness.

1. We believe in Infinite Intelligence;
2. We believe that the phenomena of Nature, both physical and spiritual, are the expression of Infinite Intelligence;
3. We affirm that a correct understanding of such expression and living in accordance therewith constitute true religion;
4. We affirm that the existence and personal identity of the individual continue after the change called death;
5. We affirm that communication with the so-called dead is a fact, scientifically proven by the phenomena of Spiritualism;

6. We believe that the highest morality is contained in the Golden Rule: "Do unto others as you would have them do unto you."

7. We affirm the moral responsibility of the individual, and that we make our own happiness or unhappiness as we obey or disobey Nature's physical and spiritual laws;

8. We affirm that the doorway to reformation is never closed against any soul here or hereafter;

9. We affirm that the Precepts of Prophecy and Healing are Divine attributes proven through Mediumship.

1. *On The Road; Or The Spiritual Investigator: A Complete Compendium Of The Science, Religion, Ethics, And Various Methods Of Investigating Spiritualism.* Melbourne: George Robertson, 1878. Section 23:47-50.
2. *Autobiography of Emma Hardinge Britten.* Edited and published by Mrs. Margaret Wilkinson. London: John Heywood, 1900. Chapter 10, p 107.

Acknowledgements

This book has been in development for longer than my life on Earth. I had to go through the entire process before I could look back, describe it, and lead other women through it.

I want to acknowledge those who helped me through the healing process over the years. I can't possibly name them all: Some are strangers; some helped in a fleeting moment; some will not realize they were essential to my healing; and some I will not have realized myself, the role they played. Some of them are: Faith, Ben, Raj, Mark, Sandie, Meredith, Brad, Kylie, Nancy, and Aunty Jean.

And those who have been key to my growth as a psychic and medium: Reverend Stephen Robinson, Reverend Seiko Obayashi, Constantina Rhodes, Reverend Georgia Marantos, and the rest of my fellow ministers at the Spiritualist Church of New York City, along with those I met and studied with at the Monroe Institute.

And I want to acknowledge those who believed without a moment's doubt that I would write a consequential book: among them are Jhancarlos, Shade, Eliza-Jane, Malado.

To the Morgan James Publishing team: Special thanks to David Hancock, CEO & Founder for believing in me and my message. To my Author Relations Manager, Bonnie Rauch, thanks for making the process seamless and easy. Many more thanks to everyone else, but especially Jim Howard, Bethany Marshall, and Nickcole Watkins.

About the Author

Reverend Stephanie Wild is a psychic medium, energy healer, and ordained Spiritualist Minister.

She is a survivor of physical, sexual, and emotional abuse, addiction, divorce, law school, and corporate America. Her professional practice is focused on helping women who have experienced sexual trauma take control of their own happiness through the art of forgiveness.

Reverend Wild works personally with clients and is also a platform medium and experienced speaker. To every engagement, she brings a visceral understanding of spiritual longing, highly developed intuitive abilities, and a passion for truth, justice, and kindness.

Reverend Wild was born and raised in Australia and now lives in New York City with her partner, two children, and Caramel Cat.

Connect with her at www.reverendwild.com.

Thank You

If you're here, you have come a long way already. Congratulations.

I would love to hear how this process is working for you; how you are applying it in your daily life and taking control of your happiness. And if you need some help successfully living without anger and resentment, please contact me for personal guidance. I am always happy to hear from my readers in any capacity.

You can visit my website, www.reverendwild.com, to learn more and set up a psychic consultation.

Love and light,
Reverend Stephanie

Morgan James
Speakers Group

We connect Morgan James published authors with live and online events and audiences who will benefit from their expertise.

Morgan James makes all of our titles available
through the Library for All Charity Organization.

www.LibraryForAll.org

9 781683 507659